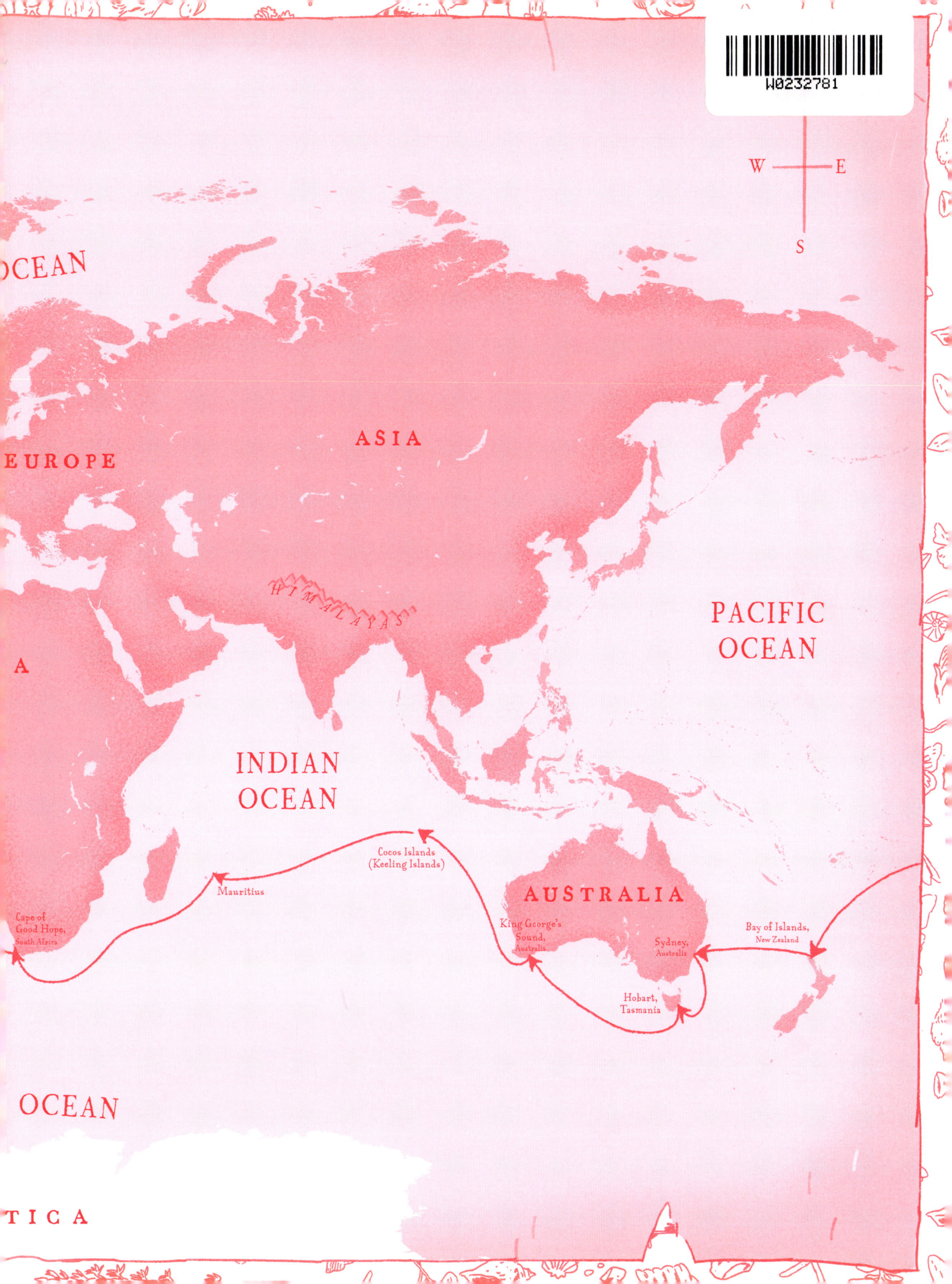

W0232781

ALEXANDRA STEWART

JOE TODD-STANTON

Darwin & Hooker

For Flora, Jake and all of Kew's mini explorers –
past, present and future. A.S

Author Acknowledgements: My huge thanks to Emily Ball, Isobel Doster, Katie Knutton and Elaine Connolly for their patience, hard work and support; also to Kew's Gina Fullerlove, Katherine Harrington, David Goyder, Julia Willison and Sharon Willoughby for their invaluable expert advice and a chance to see the amazing Joseph Hooker archive. A special thank you to Stroud School's Head of Science, Angus Reid, for his invaluable advice. My heartfelt appreciation to the brilliant Joe Todd-Stanton for his enchanting and heart-warming illustrations. Finally, a big thank you to Jonty, Flora and Jake for their endless encouragement and precious company on many happy trips to Kew.

BLOOMSBURY CHILDREN'S BOOKS
Bloomsbury Publishing Plc
50 Bedford Square, London WC1B 3DP, UK
29 Earlsfort Terrace, Dublin 2, Ireland

BLOOMSBURY, BLOOMSBURY CHILDREN'S BOOKS
and the Diana logo are trademarks of Bloomsbury Publishing Plc
First published in Great Britain 2022 by Bloomsbury Publishing Plc
Text copyright © Alexandra Stewart, 2022
Illustrations copyright © Joe Todd-Stanton, 2022

Alexandra Stewart and Joe Todd-Stanton have asserted their rights under the Copyright, Designs and Patents Act, 1988, to be identified as Author and Illustrator of this work

All rights reserved. No part of this publication may be reproduced or transmitted in any form or by any means, electronic or mechanical, including photocopying, recording, or any information storage or retrieval system, without prior permission in writing from the publishers

A catalogue record for this book is available from the British Library

ISBN: 978-1-5266-1399-8
2 4 6 8 10 9 7 5 3 1

Printed and bound in China by Leo Paper Products, Heshan, Guangdong

FSC
www.fsc.org
MIX
Paper from
responsible sources
FSC® C020056

To find out more about our authors and books visit www.bloomsbury.com
and sign up for our newsletters

The views expressed in this work are those of the author and do not necessarily reflect those of the Board of Trustees of the Royal Botanic Gardens, Kew.

Royal
Botanic Kew
Gardens

ALEXANDRA STEWART

JOE TODD-STANTON

Darwin & Hooker

A story of friendship, curiosity and
discovery that changed the world

BLOOMSBURY
CHILDREN'S BOOKS

LONDON OXFORD NEW YORK NEW DELHI SYDNEY

Introduction

I wonder if you have ever collected anything? Perhaps you have an album of football cards, a school bag jangling with key rings or a shelf stuffed with books by your favourite author? Pretty much everybody collects something – whether they realise it or not.

The heroes of our story – Charles Darwin and Joseph Hooker – were exceptional collectors and keen observers. Back in the 19th century they scoured the globe, visiting remote and dangerous places, while gathering exciting and unusual plant, animal, fossil and rock samples (called specimens) – many of which had never been seen by European scientists before. Using these extraordinary collections and observations, they were able to answer very big questions about the world around them.

As a biologist (someone who studies living things), Charles Darwin used his knowledge of the natural world to topple deeply held beliefs about how life on Earth was formed. He came to realise that all living organisms had slowly developed or 'evolved' from just one simple form of life over many, many years. Even better, he actually managed to work out how these gradual changes had taken place. He called his groundbreaking theory 'Evolution by Natural Selection', and in 1859, he wrote it down for everyone to read in a sensational book called *On the Origin of Species*.

CHARLES DARWIN

However, Charles might never have made this leap had it not been for the help and encouragement of his friends – and none more so than our story's other hero, Joseph Hooker. As a world-leading botanist (someone who studies plants) and head of the Royal Botanic Gardens, Kew, in London, Joseph collected plants from across the world to learn about why they grow where they do. He freely shared his ideas and his expertise with Charles, who used them to help develop his famous theory.

But, even more importantly, Joseph proved himself to be a brave and loyal friend; listening to, challenging and ultimately defending Charles's revolutionary ideas – at a moment in history when few would give them the time of day.

This, then, is the story of two remarkable men – whose shared passion for collecting and powerful friendship helped change our understanding of the world for ever.

JOSEPH HOOKER

PART ONE:
The Early Years

Charles Darwin: Boyhood, boarding school and beetles

CHARLES ROBERT DARWIN
FAMILY TREE

Erasmus Darwin
(1731–1802)

Mary Howard
(1740–1770)

Josiah Wedgwood
(1730–1795)

Sarah Wedgwood
(1734–1815)

Dr Robert Waring Darwin
(1766–1848)

Susannah Darwin
(1765–1817)

Marianne
(1798–1858)

Caroline
(1800–1888)

Susan
(1803–1866)

Erasmus
(1804–1881)

Charles
(1809–1882)

Catherine
(1810–1866)

Charles Robert Darwin was born on 12 February 1809, in the bustling market town of Shrewsbury in England.

Life in the Darwins' handsome red-brick home, called The Mount, was easy and comfortable. But unknown to baby 'Bobby' – the nickname his parents gave their newborn – Charles had arrived at a time when the world was going through rapid change and upheaval.

A changing world

In Europe, the French emperor, Napoleon Bonaparte, was busy trying to expand his empire through a series of wars. Across the Atlantic, a young United States of America was soon to start its own war with the United Kingdom. Meanwhile, all the around the world, Britain was using its powerful Royal Navy to increase its control and influence over other countries. This empire-building was celebrated at the time, but it had negative consequences for those people whose countries were colonised.

Back at home, Britain was in the grip of the Industrial Revolution; a time when great leaps in science and technology were transforming the way people lived, worked and thought. Towns were expanding and factories were popping up like mushrooms. Gas lights were beginning to illuminate city streets and houses, George Stephenson was soon to build the first steam locomotive and, in Italy, scientist Alessandro Volta had invented the world's first battery.

The country was seeing great changes due to the Industrial Revolution.

A forward-thinking family

Charles's own family had played a key part in this revolution. His mother's father, Josiah Wedgwood, ran a well-known pottery company that was one of the first to mass-produce ceramics in factories.

The Darwin side of the family were also a forward-thinking bunch. Charles's other grandfather was the infamous doctor, poet and philosopher, Erasmus Darwin. Erasmus had caused a stir in 1794, when he published a book called *Zoonomia*, in which he declared his belief that species (the word for a group of living things that are very similar and can reproduce together) could change, or 'evolve' over time. The theory was shocking because most British people accepted the Bible's seven-day creation story as literal truth. They believed that God had designed all living things, exactly as they now appeared, as part of a grand master plan. On the sixth day, he had created humans to rule over the rest of God's creation. Everything and everyone had their own fixed place. To question this story was to question God's very existence. Dangerously, it was also to question the hierarchy (the system of how people are ordered into different levels in society) under which British society pottered along pretty peacefully.

Wedgwood vase

Growing up

With such an interesting family, it is unsurprising that the young Charles was brought up in a lively and inquisitive household.

His father, Dr Robert Waring Darwin, was a popular and wealthy family doctor. He was a large man and, whilst he could be stern and easily angered, he was exceptionally kind.

Charles's mother, Susannah, died when he was eight and his memories of her were few and far between. Luckily, as the second youngest of six children, he had three doting and very clever older sisters to look out for him in her place. Marianne, Caroline and Susan taught, entertained and cared for their brother devotedly – even reminding a stroppy teenage Charles to wash his feet when they got too smelly!

Charles's three older sisters looked after him.

First collections

The Mount was a happy place and a busy one. There was always someone to play with or something to do. But the young Charles loved two hobbies above all else: collecting objects and studying nature. His passion for collecting was boundless and he would carefully gather up and store anything from shells, coins and pebbles, to wax seals from his father's letters.

His interest in nature was just as powerful, and he would spend hours catching newts in the local quarry pool, examining plants in the garden and exploring the Shropshire countryside. His father encouraged him, presenting Charles with his first two natural history books – one on stones, fossils and minerals and another on insects. Inspired by these books, Charles began to collect insects too.

School days

However, Charles's childhood was not all fun and games. When he was nine, he was sent to a boarding school. He hated pretty much everything about it, from the overcrowded and stinking dormitories (shared bedrooms) to the revolting food and harsh punishments. Most of all, as a budding naturalist (someone who studies plants and animals), he found the endless lessons in Classics (Latin and ancient Greek) incredibly boring.

Charles collected objects like shells, coins and pebbles.

Boarding school was boring and Charles hated it.

An education

Recognising that his son was not suited to school, Charles's father made the bold decision to send a sixteen-year-old Charles to study medicine at the University of Edinburgh.

Although he was glad to leave boarding school, Charles was frustrated to find medicine just as dreary as Classics. What's more, he found the study of the human body rather revolting.

However, all was not lost. Charles formed an important friendship with a naturalist called Dr Robert Grant. It was while Charles was helping Robert with his studies that he made his first scientific discovery – observing through his microscope how a tiny sea creature, called *Flustra*, reproduced. To many, it would have sounded unremarkable but for Charles, it was a moment of breathless excitement that would inspire a lifetime of discovery.

Flustra

Making discoveries at the University of Edinburgh.

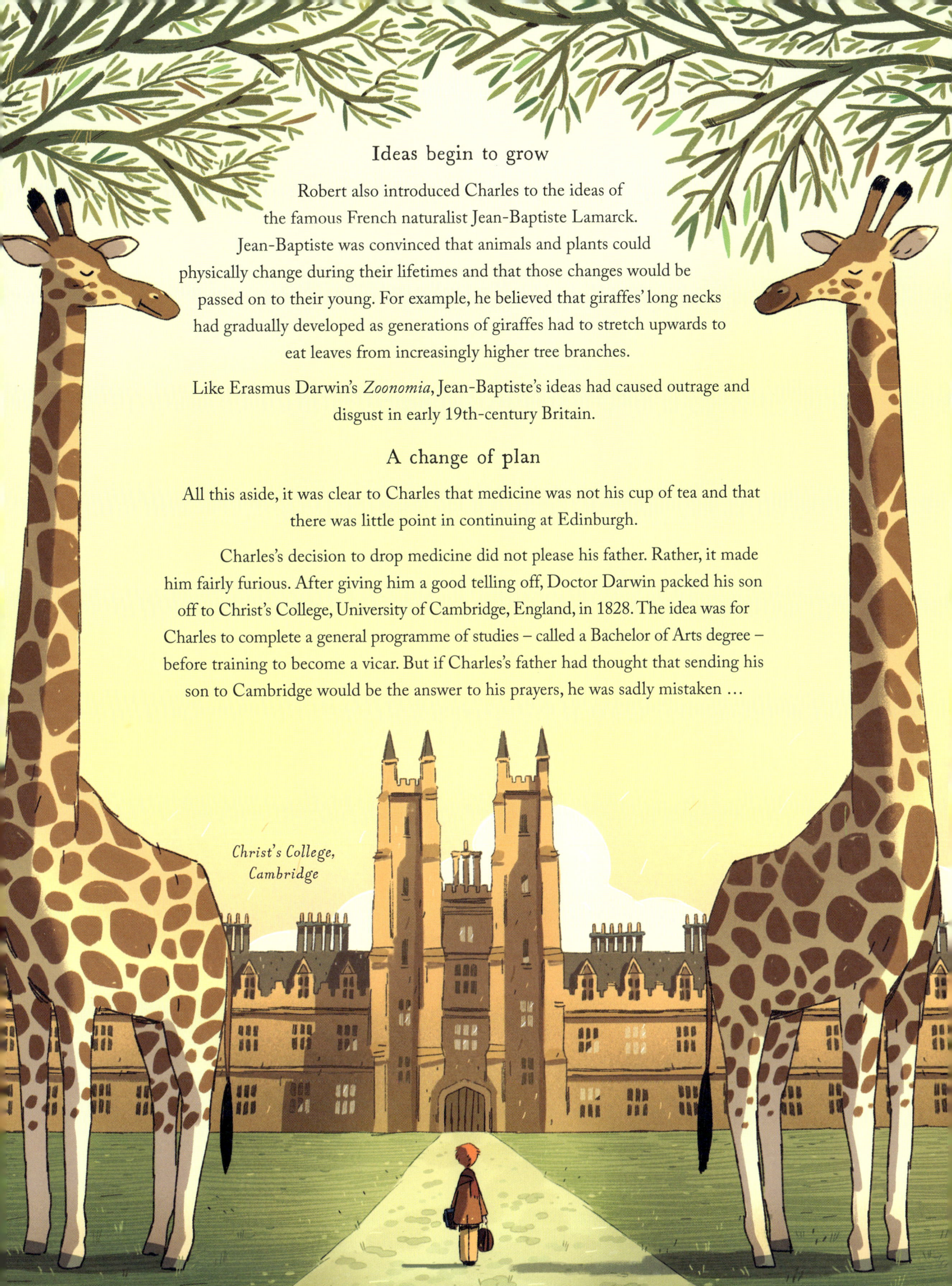

Ideas begin to grow

Robert also introduced Charles to the ideas of the famous French naturalist Jean-Baptiste Lamarck. Jean-Baptiste was convinced that animals and plants could physically change during their lifetimes and that those changes would be passed on to their young. For example, he believed that giraffes' long necks had gradually developed as generations of giraffes had to stretch upwards to eat leaves from increasingly higher tree branches.

Like Erasmus Darwin's *Zoonomia*, Jean-Baptiste's ideas had caused outrage and disgust in early 19th-century Britain.

A change of plan

All this aside, it was clear to Charles that medicine was not his cup of tea and that there was little point in continuing at Edinburgh.

Charles's decision to drop medicine did not please his father. Rather, it made him fairly furious. After giving him a good telling off, Doctor Darwin packed his son off to Christ's College, University of Cambridge, England, in 1828. The idea was for Charles to complete a general programme of studies – called a Bachelor of Arts degree – before training to become a vicar. But if Charles's father had thought that sending his son to Cambridge would be the answer to his prayers, he was sadly mistaken …

Christ's College, Cambridge

Charles at Cambridge

Charles had a whale of a time at Cambridge – but for all
the wrong reasons.

Doing as little work as possible, he spent most of his time shooting, fox
hunting and partying. He was also a proud member of the 'Glutton Club' –
a group of students who dined on birds and beasts that no sensible person
would consider eating. Foxes, badgers and hawks made it on to the menu,
but after a particularly stringy old brown owl, the members decided enough
was enough. Charles didn't know it, but he would soon be eating many more
weird and wonderful creatures in faraway lands!

Amidst all the merrymaking, Charles found time to indulge in his new
love: beetle hunting. Carrying nets, tins and boxes, he would disappear off
into the countryside for hours, searching anywhere and everywhere for new
specimens. He would stop at nothing to improve his collection, once popping
a beetle into his mouth to prevent it from escaping. Unfortunately for
Charles, the shocked beetle squirted out some foul-tasting liquid that burnt
his tongue, forcing him to spit it out. Fortunately, the beetle wasn't poisonous.

Although Charles paid little attention to his work at Cambridge, he did make some life-changing connections. Without a doubt, the most important of these was his friendship with the vicar and Professor of Botany, John Henslow. The two men were thick as thieves and Charles became a regular in the front row of Henslow's classes. Kind, warm and considerate, John nurtured Charles's interest in natural history on long walks and over dinners.

When the time came for Charles to take his final exams, he worked furiously to make up for lost time. To his father's relief, he passed them and completed his degree. With the hard work over for now, Charles was determined to do some travelling. He hoped to persuade his father to let him spend a year in Tenerife – where he would study the island's geology and wildlife. Only after that, would he settle down to train as a vicar.

Little did he realise, however, that he was about to be made an offer that would turn his life and, indeed, the whole world, upside down.

Charles enjoyed his time at Cambridge.

Joseph Hooker: Born for Botany

JOSEPH DALTON HOOKER
FAMILY TREE

Joseph Hooker
1754–1845

Lydia Vincent
1759–1829

Dawson Turner
1797–1892

Mary Palgrave
1774–1850

Sir William Jackson Hooker
1785–1865

Maria Turner
1797–1892

William Dawson
1816–1814

Maria
1819–1889

Joseph Dalton
1817–1911

Elizabeth
1820–1898

Mary Harriet
1825–1841

As Charles Darwin stood on the brink of adventure, over 500 kilometres away, in the Scottish city of Glasgow, a teenage boy was considering his own big milestone.

His name was Joseph Dalton Hooker and he was about to begin eight years of study at the University of Glasgow.

Born in Suffolk in 1817, Joseph was the second son of the famous botanist Sir William Jackson Hooker and Maria Turner, the daughter of a well-known botanist, banker and bird expert.

When Joseph was three, the family moved to Scotland, where William Hooker had taken a job as Professor of Botany at the University of Glasgow.

Brilliant botany

Botany is the study of plants. Today, we appreciate the importance of studying plants because we understand all of the many ways in which our existence depends upon them. However, at that time, most people were not interested in studying plants for their own sake, and universities simply saw them as useful ingredients for making medicines with. So, botany was not a well-respected subject – unless you lived in the Hooker household.

Joseph at his happiest – surrounded by plants.

Like father, like son

Young Joseph shared his father's passion for plants. He enjoyed collecting them and he soon became something of an expert. Old before his years, Joseph was just seven when he began going to his father's botany lectures at the university, for fun.

Although he was a hard worker, Joseph's family did not initially believe he was 'naturally' clever. However, he proved them wrong by going to university aged fourteen! Here he studied a variety of subjects, including maths and Classics, before going on to work for a degree in medicine (there was no such thing as a science degree in those days, so medicine was the next best thing). Joseph was a keen learner, once walking nearly forty kilometres to get to a lecture on time. In his spare time, he indulged his love of plants, creating his own library of dried plants – known as a 'herbarium'.

NAVAL OFFICER
J.D. HOOKER

An unusual job offer

As his time at university drew to an end, Joseph began wondering what to do with his life.

His family were not rich, like Charles Darwin's, so Joseph needed to find a job that paid well. Despite his training, he did not really fancy being a doctor, and there was little hope of a recent graduate finding a role in botany.

But Joseph was in luck. His father had friends in high places and was not afraid to make the most of them. He found Joseph a job as a ship's doctor on a Royal Naval expedition to the mysterious icy wilderness of the Antarctic.

In those days, ship's doctors (known as surgeons) often doubled as expedition naturalists – collecting and studying animals, plants and rocks during the voyage. To his delight, Joseph was made the expedition botanist, giving him a unique chance to launch himself as a plant scientist, while earning some money.

As a Royal Naval Officer, he would have to wear a uniform, follow strict ship rules and help with other duties on board. However, this was a small price to pay for the extraordinary experience he would gain.

An eager Joseph couldn't wait for his expedition to the Antarctic.

Preparing for life at sea

The expedition was due to set sail in September 1839. The weeks beforehand were a blur of activity as Joseph prepared for what would be a long and dangerous voyage into the unknown.

He spent his precious spare time poring over the pages of a gripping new book that had been given to him by a family friend. The book was an account of a young naturalist's five-year journey around the world aboard a ship. Joseph was enthralled by the exciting tales and colourful descriptions it contained. He was so eager to finish it that he slept with it under his pillow so he could read it as soon as he woke in the morning.

The book was called *The Voyage of the Beagle* and the name of the man who had written it was none other than Charles Robert Darwin ...

Charles's story of his journey around the world published in May 1839, just months before Joseph's own adventures were about to begin.

PART TWO:
Expeditions and Discovery

Darwin's voyage on the H M S *Beagle*

Charles had spent part of the summer of 1831 studying the rocks and landscape of North Wales and perfecting plans for his Tenerife project. On his return home, he found an exciting letter awaiting him from Professor Henslow.

The letter contained details of a Royal Naval expedition that was soon to set sail for South America. Its mission was to measure and map the continent's coastline – so that British ships could sail safely along it.

The project was expected to take around two years to complete and the captain of the ship, a man called Robert FitzRoy, wanted someone to keep him company along the way. However, not just anyone would do. FitzRoy wanted a well-educated gentleman who would explore and examine the wildlife, geology and geography of the many countries that his ship – the HMS *Beagle* – would visit. Charles was the ideal man for the job.

A young Charles had always dreamed of such an adventure!

Getting permission

Charles was thrilled. However, his father (who would have to pay for the escapade) was not. In his opinion, the whole thing would be an expensive and dangerous distraction. He told his son that he could only go if he could find someone else who thought it was a good idea. Clearly, he didn't think such a person existed. Fortunately for Charles, someone did – his uncle Josiah Wedgwood. Together, they confronted Robert Darwin, who, true to his word, agreed to let his son go.

Charles's dad had other plans for his son.

Departure

After weeks of delays, the *Beagle* set sail from Plymouth in December 1831. It would not return for four years, nine months and five days. Had Darwin known this at the time, he might have asked to be dropped off at the next port. A landlubber (someone unfamiliar with the sea) through and through, he was immediately struck by crippling seasickness – something he would suffer from throughout the voyage. For days on end, he could do nothing but lie miserably in his hammock.

Charles's seasickness got the better of him.

Life on board the *Beagle*

The *Beagle* was a small and fast surveying ship built in 1820.
It was 27.5m long and 7.5m wide.

There were seventy-four people squeezed on board. They included:

Charles Darwin

Captain Robert FitzRoy

Royal Marines

Darwin shared the poop cabin with two of the ship's officers. It was underneath the poop deck – a short, high deck at the back (stern) of the ship used as a high point for navigation. The name comes from the French word for stern: La Poupe.

The poop cabin was 3 m wide by 3 m long and crammed with books and a chart table. By day, Darwin and the officers would work here. By night, Darwin would sling a hammock above it to sleep.

Rations on board included: beef, pork, cocoa, tea, bread, peas, sugar and vinegar. Vinegar was used to fight scurvy – a disease caused by lack of Vitamin C.

Captain FitzRoy kept tight discipline on the ship. Sailors who disobeyed orders or were drunk and unruly were flogged (beaten) or placed in leg irons.

Royal Naval Officers and sailors

A missionary

An instrument maker

An artist

Three native South Americans*

*Yokcushlu, Elleparu and Orundellico had been kidnapped on FitzRoy's previous voyage and were being brought back to their homeland.

Scientific instruments

The *Beagle* carried a host of scientific instruments, which provided accurate information for new charts and for weather forecasting. The instruments included:

Theodolites: for measuring angles.

Barometers: to measure air pressure. Weather forecasters use barometers to predict short-term changes in the weather.

Sounding line: a length of rope with a lead weight at the end for measuring water depth.

Chronometers: (clocks) to measure time on board the ship.

Sextant: to measure the position of the Sun and stars to find the ship's location.

Arriving in South America

When the ship reached the Brazilian port of Salvador, Charles immediately began exploring the surrounding rainforest.

He was instantly entranced by the colours, sights and sounds that surrounded him – from the elegant grasses and glossy green leaves to the deafening noise made by countless insects. He had found his paradise.

Staying in Brazil, they moved on to Rio de Janeiro. Here, Charles spent more time in the rainforest, collecting a huge array of plant and animal specimens – many of which had never been documented by European naturalists before.

In one day alone, in a small patch of forest, he found sixty-eight different species of beetle. Charles was astonished by nature's endless variety and fascinated by the clever ways in which animals and plants behaved: from butterflies that communicated through clicking sounds to the high-speed flapping of hummingbirds' wings.

Charles carefully observed and recorded what he saw in his diaries and letters home. He also obsessively collected everything he could find – preserving and packing up specimens to ship back to the UK, for experts to examine and identify.

Charles felt at home observing specimens in the Brazilian rainforests.

Fossil hunting

Charles was also intrigued by the landscape around him and the secrets it held. When the ship docked at Bahía Blanca on the Argentine coast, he went fossil hunting. Digging in the cliffs, he and some of his shipmates came across a treasure trove of fossilised bones and teeth from animals that had lived long ago. Amongst them were the fossilised remains of what looked like a gigantic armadillo. Having actually eaten roasted armadillo for his tea a few days earlier, Charles recognised the creature straight away. However, Charles was baffled. This immense shelled animal was so much bigger than any armadillo he'd ever seen, or eaten!

The fossilised remains of a gigantic armadillo.

During the course of his South American adventures, he would go on to discover the fossilised remains of a number of giant mammals – all of which had become extinct many thousands of years previously. He was struck by the strong similarities between these fossils and the living animals he saw around him.

Could there be, he later wondered, a direct connection between the two?

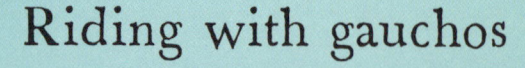

Riding with gauchos

It was not just Argentina's fossils that provided Charles with food for thought. Its legendary gauchos did too.

Gauchos are cowboys who live and work on the Argentine grasslands – called the Pampas. Charles spent some exhilarating weeks in their company galloping around on horses, sleeping under the stars and learning to catch his food.

The gauchos welcomed Charles, teaching him all about their way of life.

The matter of the rhea

One of the gauchos' favourite catches was an ostrich-like bird called a rhea. They explained to Charles that there were two different varieties of rhea – a larger 'common' one and a smaller one, with different colouring and more feathery legs. Charles was intrigued. Why, he wondered, would God bother to make two varieties of rhea that were only slightly different to one another, when surely one would do?

He was determined to hunt down the second, smaller, variety of rhea to examine it for himself. Eventually he found one – but not in the way he had hoped. One of the ship's crew had shot and cooked what Charles thought was a young common rhea. He was enjoying his dinner when he realised – to his horror – that he was eating the very thing he had been searching high and low for! Desperately he gathered up what remained of the bones and feathers to study.

When it was examined back in the UK, it was declared to be a different species to the common rhea – rather than just a different variety. It was given the scientific name *Rhea darwinii* (or Darwin's rhea) in Charles's honour.

Common rhea

Darwin's rhea

SPECIES AND VARIATION

Domestic cats and big cats are different species in the same family.

Variation

However, it is important to remember that members of the same species are not identical to one another.

Look at your friends and classmates. You are all members of the human species but some of you will have different eye colour and hair colour. Some will be taller and some will be shorter. The presence of differences between living things of the same species is called 'variation'.

Species

To help us make sense of the mind-boggling number of living things that populate our amazing planet, scientists have grouped or 'classified' them into different 'species'. A species is a group of organisms that are very similar to each other and that can breed with one another to produce fertile offspring.

You and your friends all vary from one another, despite being the same species.

The Fuegians

By the end of 1832, the *Beagle* had reached Tierra del Fuego, at the tip of South America.

FitzRoy had visited Tierra del Fuego before, on a voyage several years earlier. When he had returned to England, he had brought with him four natives from the area, whom he had kidnapped. One of his hostages tragically died of smallpox not long after arriving. The remaining three, a young girl called Yokcushlu, and two young men called Elleparu and Orundellico, were re-named Fuegia Basket, Jemmy Button and York Minister. They were given 'fine' clothes, taught what FitzRoy considered to be 'polite' English manners and even taken to meet the king and queen. They were also forced to learn about and practise the Christian faith. FitzRoy hoped that when he returned them to their community, they would spread their new religion and 'civilised' way of living.

FitzRoy tried to 'civilise' the Fuegians by dressing them in fine English clothing ...

On returning Yokcushlu, Elleparu and Orundellico to their home, Charles was shocked by the difference between them and their fellow Fuegians. As the *Beagle* pulled slowly into shore, he was struck by the naked bodies, uncut hair and piercing cries of those awaiting their arrival. Although this behaviour might have seemed strange to FitzRoy, Charles and the rest of the crew, to the Fuegians it was, of course, entirely normal. They just lived a different way of life.

When the *Beagle* crew returned to Tierra del Fuego eighteen months later to see how FitzRoy's 'project' was working out, they discovered that the trio had abandoned their 'new' way of life and were living exactly as they had before. It showed Charles that expensive clothes and fancy manners were next to useless to the people of Tierra del Fuego. The experience affected Charles deeply. Although the Bible said that humans were superior to other animals, it was clear to him that, once you stripped away the 'fine' clothes and 'polite' manners, we are very much part of the natural world.

It's hard to believe it now, but FitzRoy thought he was doing his hostages, and the tribes from which they came, a favour by introducing them to a 'better' way of life. His attitude reflected the way Europeans thought about the rest of the world at that time. Today, of course, we can see the 'project' for what it really was: a cruel experiment rooted in false and dangerous ideas.

... but when they were set free, they soon returned to their own way of life.

The Earth moves

In June 1834, two and a half years after it set sail, the *Beagle* reached the Pacific Ocean and headed northwards along the Chilean coast. Here, more surprises lay in wait.

During his downtime on board the *Beagle*, Charles had been carefully reading a book written by the geologist (someone who studies the Earth) Charles Lyell. Lyell – who would later become Charles's good friend – believed that the Earth's surface had been shaped by gradual changes that had occurred over a vast period of time. If he was right, the Earth was far older than the 6,000 years that Christians – using information in the Bible's Old Testament – had calculated it to be. Whilst climbing in Chile's high Andes mountains, Charles found fossilised seashells that had once lain at the bottom of the sea. Here, before his eyes, was proof that the seabed had been pushed up, bit by bit, over countless years (far more than just 6,000), to form mountains.

Not only that, Charles got to experience for himself how this kind of momentous change happened. While in Chile, he felt the ground tremble violently as a devastating earthquake hit the region. In the aftermath, Charles was amazed to discover that rocks with live seashells still attached to them had been lifted permanently above the tide line. When FitzRoy got his measuring instruments out, he discovered that the level of the land had risen by around three metres. This was exactly the kind of geological change Lyell was talking about.

Fossil hunting in the Andes mountains.

The Galápagos Islands

Of all the incredible places Charles visited, the most monumental stop was in September 1835, when the *Beagle* visited a small group of rocky islands, called the Galápagos Islands.

Around 1,000 km off the coast of Ecuador, the Galápagos Islands had been formed by a series of volcanic eruptions. The oldest of the islands were created roughly three million years ago – which is no age at all when you consider that the Earth is over four billion years old.

The islands teemed with extraordinary and unique wildlife. Whilst many of the plants and animals had similarities to those on the South American mainland, there were some that were like nothing Charles had seen before. Swarms of large iguanas clung to the rocks on the beach, slipping into the water every now and again to feed. Charles was fascinated by their eating habits – knowing of no other lizard that searched for food in the sea.

*Marine
iguana*

Equally enthralling were the islands' unusual birds. Bold blue-footed boobies and yellow warblers hopped right up to Charles – completely unafraid. On one of his walks, Charles came face-to-face with a giant tortoise chewing on a cactus. When he measured its shell, he found it had a two-metre circumference. The Galápagos tortoises were so big that he was able to hitch a lift on the back of one as it plodded up a hill to find water! They were remarkable creatures – but not remarkable enough to stop Charles and his shipmates from feasting on them.

What made the Galápagos even more intriguing was the fact that its wildlife differed from island to island. For instance, the tortoises on each island had different-shaped shells. But what fascinated Charles the most were the finches. These little birds were pretty similar in shape, size and colour – but each had a different beak, depending upon which island they inhabited. The beak, he noticed, was cleverly shaped to help the finch find and eat the kind of food that was available on its specific island. In total, Charles counted thirteen different types of finches.

Helped by his personal servant, Syms Covington, Charles feverishly collected and preserved as much as he could for later inspection. For now, there was the rest of the voyage to think about …

Giant tortoise

Blue-footed booby

Australia, New Zealand and Tahiti

The *Beagle* sailed westwards across the Pacific, stopping in Tahiti and New Zealand before heading to Australia.

Here, again, Charles marvelled at a whole host of peculiar species found nowhere else on Earth. The curious-looking duck-billed platypus particularly fired his imagination. Whilst watching several playing in a pond one evening, he noticed how they behaved like the water voles he knew so well from home. The way they swam, dived and burrowed into the side of a bank when danger approached was just the same.

Why, he wondered, would an all-powerful God go to all the fuss and bother of creating the water vole for Europe and North America and the platypus for Australia? Why didn't he just create one species and place it all over the world?

Pondering these strange yet familiar creatures, Charles couldn't help but think of home. Despite Australia's curious wildlife and breathtaking beauty, he longed for England's shores. When the *Beagle* left Australia in March 1836, he was more than ready to call time on his epic adventure.

Same but different – Australia's duck-billed platypus ...

... and Europe's water vole.

Back in England

The *Beagle* zigzagged slowly back towards Falmouth, England arriving on 2 October 1836.

Brimming with joy and relief, Charles left the ship and immediately boarded a horse-drawn coach bound for Shropshire. Finally, five years and three days after he had left, an exhausted but excited Charles arrived home, just in time for breakfast. As he tucked into his bacon and eggs, recent meals of tortoise soup and roasted armadillo must have already seemed a world away.

A lot had changed since a young Charles had set off on his adventure.

Although the dogs greeted him like he had only left the day before, much had changed whilst Charles had been gone. Towns had grown, more factories had sprung up and mile upon mile of railway track had been laid across Britain. Family and friends had grown older, some had married and some now had children. But perhaps the greatest change had happened to Charles himself.

Professor Henslow had been working hard on Charles's behalf, sharing Charles's discoveries with fellow scientists. To Charles's delight, his fossil, plant and animal collections and his geological observations had caused quite a stir amongst the experts of the day.

Charles had left England as a young graduate with vague plans to become a vicar. He returned, aged twenty-seven, determined to take his place among the leading men of science. However, nobody in 1836 could possibly have guessed quite how distinguished that place would be.

Ideas begin to grow

After years on the move, Charles now had the space and time to mull over the many weird and wonderful things he had seen.

As well as gathering 1,500 species bottled in spirits and almost 4,000 skins, bones and other dried specimens, Charles had written 2,000 pages of notes on geology and zoology. It would take years to sort, identify and catalogue everything. On top of this, he set to work on an official account of his travels, which would become *The Voyage of the Beagle*. As he worked, his brain bubbled away with countless questions …

Charles worked day in, day out, to make sense of his findings.

Despite what the Bible said, all of the evidence seemed to suggest that life on Earth had not been created exactly as humans now found it. It seemed to Charles that species gradually changed and evolved from one into another. What's more, they had been doing so over billions of years, because Earth was clearly far older than Christians believed.

Charles began thinking through his ideas and writing them down in a series of secret notebooks – now called the 'Transmutation Notebooks'. Transmutation means changing from one thing into another.

In one of his notebooks, Charles drew a diagram of a 'Tree of Life' that illustrated his belief that all life on Earth had evolved from just one common ancestor. At the bottom of Charles's 'tree' were the most ancient and simple life forms, such as bacteria. As the tree ascended, increasingly complicated descendants, such as ferns, flowering plants, fungi, molluscs and mammals, branched off along the trunk.

Charles's 'Tree of Life' diagram

However, if Charles's hunch was correct, there were still vital pieces missing from the puzzle. What he really needed to know was *why* species evolved and *how*.

The missing piece of the puzzle

The answer came to Charles in the autumn of 1838, when he read an essay by the demographer (someone who studies populations) Thomas Malthus.

In the essay, Malthus argued that the world's human population was prevented from growing out of control by famine, disease and war. Whenever any of these disasters struck, only the strongest survived.

Charles knew that the same thing happened to all other animals and plants. Parents produced many more offspring than could ever reach adulthood. Only the strongest – those best equipped to deal with the challenges of their environment – would win the battle to survive. Charles called this process 'natural selection' and realised it was the key that unlocked the mystery of evolution.

But how, exactly, did it all work?

EVOLUTION BY NATURAL SELECTION

Remember the finches Charles found on the Galápagos Islands? Their story is a fascinating example of how species evolve and new ones are created, thanks to the power of natural selection.

There are thirteen different species of finch on the Galápagos Islands. Some of these species only live on certain islands and each species differs slightly from the others. The clearest difference is in the size and shape of their beaks, which are especially suited to the types of food they eat on the island where they live.

*The **green warbler finch** has a fine, needle-like beak that it uses to probe for insects.*

*The **large ground finch** has a big, stout beak that it uses to crack open large, tough seeds.*

*The **woodpecker finch** has a large, strong beak it uses to root out beetle larvae from cracks in trees. It can also use twigs held in its beak as tools to dislodge larvae from cracks and crevices.*

*The **cactus finch** has a long, sharp beak that it uses to extract seeds from cactus fruit.*

Although each of these finches are different species, they all descended from one species of finch found on the South American mainland. But why did they change so much? And how did these changes take place?

Warbler finch

6

4b *On islands with insects, finches that can grasp sticks are more likely to survive than finches that can't grasp them.*

4

Some finches have slightly longer, slimmer beaks that are good for catching and eating grubs and insects.

4

Small tree finch

6

The surviving finches produce their own offspring, passing on their useful characteristics.

4

Certain characteristics prove useful for eating the different food on each island.

5 The finches settle and have chicks. Those born with the best characteristics for their island are more likely to survive.

Small ground finch

6

7 Eventually, over many years, the finches on each island evolve to become different species with unique characteristics.

Ground finch

6

4a *On islands with nuts and hard-shelled seeds, finches with stout beaks are more likely to survive than those with thinner, finer beaks.*

4

Some finches have slightly stronger or stouter beaks that are good for crushing nuts and seeds.

Larvae ③

Insects ③

③ Each island has different habitats and food sources.

Some finches fly to different islands. ②

Seed-eating finch

Soft-shelled seed ③

Hard-shelled seed ③

Evolution by Natural Selection
How the new species of finch formed

Seed-eating finches arrive on one of the Galápagos Islands.

1 Around two million years ago, a single population of seed-eating finches from the South American mainland arrived on one of the Galápagos Islands.

2 The population steadily grew and, eventually, some of the more adventurous finches flew off to live on the other islands.

3 Each of the islands had different habitats and food sources. Some had a plentiful supply of soft-shelled seeds and others had a greater supply of hard-shelled seeds. Some islands offered a better supply of insects or insect larvae for the birds to eat.

4 On each island, certain characteristics proved more useful than others in the birds' struggle to find food and survive.

4a On an island where hard-shelled seeds were the main food source, a bird with a stouter beak was more likely to survive than one with a smaller, thinner beak that could not crack the hard shells.

4b On an island where insects and larvae were more plentiful, a bird that could grasp a twig in its beak and use it to dig insects and larvae out of rotten wood, would have a better chance of surviving than one that couldn't.

5 The finches settled on their new islands, mated and had babies (offspring). Just like humans, each baby finch was different from its siblings. Purely by chance, some chicks in a family would inherit useful characteristics from their parents – giving them an advantage in the struggle for survival on their island.

6 The chicks that had inherited useful characteristics would live long enough to produce offspring and pass these characteristics on to a new generation. Their unlucky offspring that weren't so well adapted to their habitat, would not. This was natural selection in action.

7 Over many, many generations, the tiny changes brought about by natural selection added up to become big ones and the finches became distinct species.

Charles called this 'Evolution by Natural Selection'.

Gathering the evidence

Now came the really hard part – finding the evidence to back up the theory.

Charles set to work gathering facts, testing arguments, conducting experiments, questioning experts and carefully noting everything down in his 'Transmutation Notebooks'. It was a process that would go on for the next twenty years.

For now, he kept his work a tightly held secret. This was for a very good reason. Charles knew that what he was suggesting would cause uproar within Victorian society and the scientific community. Before he could unveil his theory, he had to make sure it was watertight.

Charles gets married

While all this had been going on, Charles had been pondering another difficult, but more practical, question: whether or not he should try to find a wife.

In 1839, he married his cousin, Emma Wedgwood. Emma was a patient, kind-hearted and intelligent woman and supported Charles in his work.

Over the next few years, Charles was completely absorbed in his studies. However, to his great frustration, he was frequently interrupted by episodes of a mystery illness that had plagued him since his return to England. He could be out of action for days on end. Although he saw a host of doctors, not one could work out what the cause was, or how to cure it.

Emma and Charles on their wedding day

The Voyage of the Beagle

Nevertheless, Charles's mood lifted that summer when his book about the voyage of the *Beagle* was published. It was an instant hit with the public and his fellow scientists. Charles was overjoyed.

Emma was a kind and doting wife who took care of Charles.

Hooker meets Darwin

Charles becoming a published author was not the only momentous event of the summer.

Whilst strolling in London's Trafalgar Square one day, he bumped into an old shipmate from the *Beagle*. The shipmate introduced him to his companion – a young wiry man with glasses. The man told him that he was about to depart on a long trip to Antarctica. His name was Joseph Hooker.

It was fair to say that the meeting made more of an impact on Joseph than it did on Charles. After all, Charles was already a well-known scientific figure, whilst Joseph was just a lowly ship's doctor. What's more, Joseph had been busily reading all about Charles's *Beagle* adventures as he prepared for his own. He must have been starstruck to meet his hero.

Neither of them knew it at the time, but this fleeting introduction would evolve into one of science's most important friendships.

Trafalgar Square, London

Hooker's Antarctic adventure

Not quite knowing the importance of this meeting just yet, Joseph had little time to ponder the future. His mind was focussed on his impending journey to the frozen south.

The ship that would take him there was a sturdy wooden vessel called HMS *Erebus*. Originally a bomb ship, designed to fire explosives at enemy coastal defences, it was as tough as nails – ideal for sailing in icy waters.

Commanded by the highly-experienced Captain James Clark Ross, the crew of *Erebus* and her sister ship, HMS *Terror*, were tasked with finding the South Magnetic Pole. The magnetic poles are the areas on the Earth's surface – one near the Geographic North Pole and one near the Geographic South Pole – where the Earth's magnetic fields are strongest. James had already located the North Magnetic Pole during an expedition to the Arctic, in 1831.

North Pole

South Pole

Geographic
North Pole

North
Magnetic
Pole

The journey south

The *Erebus* and the *Terror* set sail on 30 September 1839. As they headed south, they called at islands along their route. During these stopovers Joseph had the chance to clamber ashore and examine the plant life.

On the Cape Verde Islands, west of Africa, he was excited to see tropical vegetation for the first time in his life. Meanwhile, on the desolate Kerguelen Islands, just outside the Antarctic Circle, Joseph found a large and mysterious cabbage-like plant that the ships' cooks added to their soups.

Like Charles, Hooker was constantly observing and writing down his findings.

How, he wondered, had this peculiar plant got to this remote island? And what was its relationship to similar plants found on other continents? It was this kind of cabbagey conundrum that sparked Joseph's lifelong interest in plant geography (the study of where vegetation grows and why). What were the scientific laws that explained why particular plants grew in particular places? He would spend the rest of his days searching the world for the answers.

These were exactly the kinds of questions that Charles Darwin was asking too. And, just as Charles had done, Joseph carefully observed and collected as many specimens as he could lay his hands on.

At sea

Whilst at sea, Joseph busied himself with a series of tasks: treating sick sailors, taking readings, preparing weather tables and examining the marine life caught in the ship's tow nets. Sitting at a table in the captain's cabin, with a microscope, pencil and paper, a contented Joseph would skilfully draw the plants and animals he had found in the net and on the islands.

Hooker at work on the Erebus.

A spell of bad weather

The journey wasn't all plain sailing though. As the ships headed further south, Joseph got a taste of just how dangerous things could get. At the end of July, there was a terrible gale. A sailor was hit by a sail, fell into the sea and drowned. Four men sent out in a boat to save him were washed overboard, nearly perishing in the freezing water. Meanwhile, the *Erebus* and *Terror* became separated in the chaos.

As the *Erebus* sailed on alone, it ran into a hurricane that stripped off its sails and smashed its lifeboats. Eventually it reached Hobart, Tasmania, where it was reunited with the *Terror*.

The Antarctic Circle

It was over a year since the *Erebus* and the *Terror* had left England and it was now time to head to their main destination : Antarctica.

On New Year's Day 1841, they crossed the Antarctic Circle, reaching a band of pack ice (a large mass of ice floating in the sea) a few days later. It took an hour of hurling the *Erebus* repeatedly at the edge of the pack before the ships broke in. A week later, they passed through the ice into open polar sea and into a region that only a handful of people had visited before.

In this perilous frozen expanse, there was no plant life for Joseph to examine. But there was more than enough to occupy him – including simply staying alive. Later that month, he slipped and fell into the icy water whilst the crew were landing on an island they had found, called Franklin Island. Almost crushed between the boat and the rocks, he was lucky to escape alive.

Sailing onwards, the ships eventually came across a towering, vertical wall of ice that stretched as far as the eye could see. This huge barrier, which we now call the Ross Ice Shelf, was impossible to sail through or around. Unable to go any further south and afraid of becoming trapped over winter in the freezing sea, the ships headed back to Tasmania.

The crew managed to make the most of out of their tricky situation.

In December, the ships set out for Antarctica once again. This time, they were not so lucky and, a few days before Christmas, they found themselves trapped in the pack ice, drifting helplessly.

Not to be beaten, they made the best of bad times. Tying their ships to a flat ice floe (a large piece of floating ice), the men set about carving mini villages out of the ice in preparation for Christmas and New Year celebrations. Snow was cut into pathways and rooms with seats were dug out, where the crew could drink, eat and dance. The more skilful craftsmen created giant ice sculptures – including a two-metre tall Sphinx. Thrones were built for the captains and a course was constructed so that the ships' pigs could be raced against one another. There was even a greasy pole for sailors to try and climb.

New Year 1842 was welcomed with music, games, dancing and feasting. The local penguin population had never seen anything quite like it.

With the festivities over, the ships returned to the task of finding a way out of the pack ice. At long last, after forty-six days, they escaped its clutches. However, their relief was short-lived when, not long after, the *Terror* crashed into the *Erebus* as it tried to dodge an iceberg in the dark. The *Erebus* was badly damaged and, after it was quickly patched up, the ships sailed to the Falkland Islands for repair.

Homeward bound

After all this danger and adventure, Joseph grew weary of his Antarctic travels and was desperate to return home.

He was secretly delighted when a third attempt to head south was scuppered by bad weather. Forced to abandon the mission, the ship headed back to England.

Finally, more than four years after setting off, the *Erebus* and *Terror* arrived home in September 1843. In an incredible feat of bravery and endurance, the crew had sailed further south than any European had ever been. And, whilst they had not reached the South Magnetic Pole, using their measurements, they had managed to calculate where it lay. A grateful Joseph hopped off the *Erebus* at London's Woolwich docks, ready to dedicate the rest of his life to botany.

A weary Joseph finally returned home.

The Hookers and the Royal Botanic Gardens, Kew

Back in England, things had taken an interesting turn for Joseph's father. In 1841, he had become Director of the Royal Botanic Gardens, Kew – a world-famous garden in London that today boasts the largest and most diverse plant and fungi collections in the world. Once the stomping ground of the royal family, the gardens had recently come under government control. William Hooker immediately set about transforming Kew into a site of botanical excellence dedicated to the collection, cultivation and study of plants from around the world.

Despite his new and important post, William was unable to offer his son a job. He was, however, able to pull a few strings on his behalf. A relieved Joseph was told he would continue receiving his Naval pay whilst settling down to write a book about the botanical collections – and 8,000 specimens – he had gathered during his expedition.

The Palm House, Royal Botanic Gardens, Kew

An unexpected letter

Joseph's bags were barely unpacked when he received a happy surprise. It was a letter from Charles Darwin, whom he had met so fleetingly in Trafalgar Square more than four years previously. Chatty and warm, Charles congratulated Joseph on his voyage and asked him if he would examine his Galápagos plants.

Although he had more than enough work to be getting on with, it was an offer Joseph could not refuse. He wrote back to accept.

This letter was to become the second of 1,400 letters that would shuttle back and forth between the two men over the next forty years.

Joseph was delighted to receive a letter from someone he admired so much.

47

PART THREE:
Friendship and Scientific Progress

Down House, Charles and Emma's home in Kent, England

Darwin's ideas evolve

Charles had not let the grass grow under his feet whilst Joseph had been away.

In between spells of sickness, he had spent a lot of time working on his theory and writing letters to anyone who might help him. He collected experts and their opinions as eagerly as he collected specimens. Whether it was professors and diplomats or Welsh sheep farmers and rabbit breeders, Charles considered nobody too grand or too humble to have their brains picked.

At the end of 1839, he and Emma had also welcomed their first child – William Erasmus Darwin. Three girls, Anne, Mary and Henrietta, arrived close behind. In total, the Darwins would have ten children, three of whom would sadly die before reaching adulthood.

In search of more space for their growing troop, Charles and Emma had moved out of London in 1842. They had settled into a large home, called Down House, in a quiet village in the county of Kent. Here, Charles enjoyed country rambles, conducting experiments in his gardens and greenhouses and beavering away in his cluttered but cosy study.

Confessing a murder

It was whilst sitting in his new study, in January 1844, that Charles plucked up the courage to write a top-secret letter to his new friend, Joseph Hooker.

In the letter, Charles declared his belief that species could change, and that he had discovered the secret of how it all happened. He likened his admission to 'confessing a murder' – and to him, it really was that serious.

It was the first time that Charles had shared his new theory with anyone. With his heart in his mouth, he sealed up the letter and posted it before he could change his mind. There was nothing he could do now but wait.

Charles trusted Joseph above anyone else.

Hooker supports Darwin

Joseph's reply, when it came, sent a wave of relief washing over Charles. Although Joseph was not yet convinced that species could change, he was keen to know more about Charles's theory.

It was the best news Charles could have hoped for. Here was someone he could rely on to challenge and advise him, but not judge. From this point onwards, Joseph became Charles's most trusted confidant.

So deep was his respect for his new friend that in 1844, a sickly Charles left secret instructions that Joseph should help edit the outline of his theory for publication should he suddenly die. What's more, it was Joseph who became the first of Charles's friends to see and comment on the outline, three years later.

A WORD OF WARNING

Later that year, an anonymously written book was published, making the case for the evolution of living things. Many readers blasted it as foul and filthy. It was a forewarning of what Charles could expect if he should go public with his theory, and a reminder that there was still much work to be done before he could make that leap.

Society was still not ready to entertain the idea of evolution.

Various plants unique to the Galápagos Islands

The botanist's perspective

One of Charles's major pieces of evidence was his collection of Galápagos plants. The energetic Joseph finished examining them in 1845. To Charles's delight, half of the 200 species Joseph identified could only be found in the Galápagos Islands and many of these were unique to single islands.

Charles's theory could explain why. The plants had arrived from the mainland, as seeds, many hundreds of thousands of years previously – probably carried in bird poo, washed up by the sea or blown by the wind. After arriving at the various Galápagos Islands, they had germinated and multiplied. Bit by bit, they had adapted to different habitats on different islands. Eventually, after many years, they had changed so much they had become different species.

Darwin's barnacles

But Joseph provided more than just practical help. He also got Charles thinking about what more he should be doing to back up his theory. In one letter, Joseph told Charles that scientists shouldn't express opinions on species if they hadn't studied and identified many species themselves.

Stung into action, Charles began a meticulous eight-year study of tiny sea creatures called barnacles. Through this, he was able to track how an entire group of organisms had evolved into different species over time. Joseph helped Charles examine his barnacle collection under the microscope and he carefully drew what they saw.

Charles's impressive barnacle collection

The closest of friends

As a regular visitor to Down House, Joseph grew used to Charles's working routines and joined him when he could.

After breakfast, the pair would head to the study where Charles would sit in his horsehair chair and bombard Joseph with botanical questions. After twenty minutes, an exhausted Charles would need to rest.

Before lunch the pair would go walking. They would inspect Charles's experiments in his greenhouses and then complete a few circuits of a gravel track – called the Sandwalk – near Down House. This was where Charles came, without fail, twice a day, to walk and think.

In the evening the pair would just enjoy each other's company. They would read books, listen to music and talk.

Part of the family

Both men found their time together useful, stimulating and hugely enjoyable. They learnt a great deal from one another and enjoyed gossiping and teasing each other.

The Darwin children loved Joseph too – whether it was feasting on gooseberries with him in the Down House kitchen or laughing as he waggled his furry eyebrows at them, he was always a welcome visitor.

Joseph was always welcome at Down House.

Hooker's Himalayan quest

But as much as Joseph loved his time at Down House and valued his friendship with Charles, the pressing need for a job and more money was about to tear them apart.

Joseph had published the first part of his *Botany of the Antarctic Voyage* – or *Flora Antarctica* – in 1844 to much praise. There were three more parts to come, but he simply was not earning enough to live on.

Coming to the rescue, Joseph's father arranged for his son to travel to India where he would collect plants for Kew, take measurements and draw maps to help the British understand this part of their empire – including areas already well known to the peoples of the Himalayas.

After arriving in Kolkata (then called Calcutta) in January 1848, Joseph travelled north by elephant, palanquin (a box carried by men) and boat. Along the way, he and his companions kept a wary eye out for tigers, bears, crocodiles and robbers.

On his long and dangerous journey, Joseph was able to learn more about Indian plants and wildlife.

Eventually, he reached Darjeeling, a town in the very north-east of India, nestled in the Himalayan foothills. From here, he made trips into the surrounding mountains to collect plants, venturing into areas no person from Europe had visited before. He was helped along the way by local men and boys – called Lepchas – who had knowledge of the region and its wildlife.

An extreme adventure

The expeditions were punishing. Joseph and his team would march for up to nine hours a day through thick forests, up and down steep mountainsides and across rickety bamboo bridges spanning raging rivers.

Along the way, they were attacked by leeches, sand flies, ticks and mosquitoes. As they climbed higher, Joseph was struck by crippling altitude sickness – which brought on a series of symptoms, such as headaches, nausea and dizziness.

The camps were not much of a refuge. Joseph's tent was a blanket thrown over the limb of a tree, which provided little protection from the rain, snow and freezing temperatures. What's more, food was often in short supply and so he became very thin. His only luxuries were an occasional cigar and the company of a dog that he had adopted called Kinchin.

Ignoring the discomfort, and with Kinchin curled at his feet, a determined Joseph spent his evenings drawing maps, labelling specimens and writing his journal and letters – all by candlelight.

Kinchin kept Joseph company as he braved freezing temperatures in the name of science.

Hooker gets to work

There was much work to be done. Thousands of plants that were new to Joseph had caught his eye – all of which needed collecting and examining.

They included many species of rhododendron that covered the mountainsides.

Joseph was also amazed to find a red and orange lichen (a type of organism made up of a fungus and an algae) growing at 5,791 metres, which he had last seen on an Antarctic island.

Lichen

Rhododendron

Joseph was lucky to get out unharmed, as his crime would normally have been met with much more dire consequences.

Joseph finds trouble

Needless to say, Joseph shared these findings with Charles in his letters home. The two wrote constantly, with Charles firing endless questions at his friend about the wildlife, climate and people of the region. Joseph did his very best to answer each one.

It seemed there was no trouble to which Joseph would not go in the name of science. Things got out of hand in 1849, when he was thrown in jail by the ruler, or Rajah, of Sikkim (a small state bordering India), having slipped over Sikkim's border without asking permission. A sheepish Joseph was eventually released unharmed, but not before the British had threatened to invade Sikkim.

Older, wiser and with around 7,000 species of plant in tow, Joseph eventually made it back to England in 1851.

Back on British soil

After so much excitement, it was time for Joseph to settle down. He was paid a decent sum of money to write up his findings from his travels, which meant that he could afford to marry his fiancée, Frances Henslow, in July 1851. Frances was also a botanist, and the daughter of Charles's Cambridge friend, Professor Henslow. She supported him with his studying and writing, which remained top of his list of priorities – despite the thrill of being a newlywed.

There was also his friendship with Charles – which would always be a priority too. By now, Charles needed Joseph's companionship more than ever. Not long after Joseph had returned to England, the Darwins' eldest daughter, nine-year-old Annie, had died of an unknown illness. Decades later, memories of his 'most sweet and affectionate child' would still reduce him to tears. He would never recover from her loss, but having his 'dear Hooker' back by his side provided some comfort amidst his despair.

Joseph and Frances

The two friends shared a deep bond and looked out for one another.

Close connections

As well as being a shoulder to cry on, Joseph was also an important sounding board for Charles when it came to his work. He was nearing the end of his barnacle study and was keen to get back to his species work. He wanted Joseph close at hand as he tried to draw it to some kind of conclusion, once and for all.

Natural selection : evidence and experiments

So started a flurry of activity, during which Down House became the epicentre of all sorts of elaborate experiments.

The weirdest of these were designed to show that plant seeds and animals could travel huge distances and still produce offspring at the end of it. If Charles could not prove this, then people would continue to argue that God had put them there.

Helped by his eager children and a sceptical Joseph, Charles placed seeds in saltwater tanks for weeks on end, to mimic them being carried across the oceans. He was delighted to discover that most of them sprouted afterwards.

Charles's experiments, though strange, were always met with enthusiasm from his children!

In another, rather gruesome experiment, he cut the feet off dead ducks and placed them in a water tank containing fresh water snails. After counting the numbers of snails that clung to them, he then waved the feet in the air to simulate flying. Once again, he was impressed by the results – many of the snails stubbornly clung on and survived. Charles considered very little too outrageous to try.

Pigeon fancier

When he wasn't experimenting, Charles continued writing to people around the world - asking questions and gathering information.

Among those who provided him with some of his most important evidence were people who kept and bred pigeons, also known as 'pigeon-fanciers'. By choosing birds with particular features to mate with one another, the pigeon fancying community had created hundreds of different varieties of pigeon. These birds came in all shapes, colours and sizes but, crucially, all of them had originated from just one pigeon, called a rock dove.

Artificial selection at work

ROCK DOVE

If breeders could change how a single species looked, in captivity, over hundreds of years, then surely nature could develop entirely new species – through natural selection – over millions of years? Charles called what the breeders were doing 'artificial selection' (something artificial is made or produced by humans rather than happening naturally), and he started collecting pigeons so that he could have a go at it himself.

Eventually the experimenting needed to stop and the proper writing had to start. So, in 1856, after twenty years of thinking about it, Charles sat down to write his theory of natural selection in as much detail as possible.

Hooker's career starts to soar

While all of this had been going on, Joseph had also been busy.

In 1853, Frances had given birth to their first child, William Henslow Hooker. He was the first of seven mini Hookers – three daughters and three more sons would follow.

In 1854, his *Himalayan Journals* were published, with a dedication to Charles at the start. Just as exciting was his appointment, a year later, as Assistant Director of the Royal Botanic Gardens, Kew. Working alongside his father, it was his job to help run the gardens – which had grown hugely since William Hooker's arrival. Now stretching over 300 acres and open to the public each afternoon, the site had more than twenty glasshouses, over 4,500 living plant species and an impressive herbarium.

The Royal Botanic Gardens, Kew, in the 1850s

The new job was a big step up for Joseph, but he still found time to help Charles – advising him on experiments and sending him packets of seeds from Kew's collection to work with. In autumn 1856, Charles gave Joseph a part of his manuscript that dealt with plant geography to read and comment on. Joseph was very impressed – he understood Charles's theory and, more importantly, he was now fully convinced that it was true.

With his friend's support, an even more confident Charles ploughed on with his writing, aiming to make it as perfect as it could be.

But something was about to happen that would throw his plans into a devastating tailspin.

Pipped at the post

In June 1858, a parcel arrived for Charles.

It had been sent from a tropical island halfway around the world by an explorer, naturalist and wildlife collector called Alfred Russel Wallace. Charles hoped the package might contain some useful snippets of information to ponder over. You can only imagine his horror when he discovered it contained an essay on evolution that was almost exactly the same as his own theory. After two decades of hard work, he had been pipped at the post.

The bottom had just fallen out of Charles's world.

What should he do now? Betraying Wallace by publishing his own theory first was out of the question. But so was writing off the last twenty years. Sick to the stomach, he turned to his friends – Joseph Hooker and geologist Charles Lyell – for advice.

They both agreed that there was only one thing for it – he and Wallace should announce their theory together. It was not how Charles had imagined things would happen, but it would have to do.

Alfred Russel Wallace

Coming up against many hurdles, Charles was lucky to have so many friends he could turn to.

Presenting the theory

The historic event took place on 1 July 1858 at a meeting of London's Linnaean Society – an organisation dedicated to the study of natural history.

After such a build-up, it was a huge anticlimax for poor Charles. He remained at home, ill and grieving the recent loss of his eighteen-month-old son, Charles Junior, from scarlet fever. Meanwhile, Wallace was still overseas.

Instead, the authors were represented by Joseph Hooker and Charles Lyell. At the end of a long evening, parts of Darwin's manuscript and Wallace's essay were read aloud by the Society's president, Thomas Bell. As Bell reached the final full stop, the earthquake that Charles had been bracing himself for failed to strike. There was barely a murmur or even a cough among the thirty or so scientists who had stayed to listen. Perhaps they had not fully grasped the importance of what they had just heard? Bell himself later complained that there had been no striking discoveries in 1858. It was a remark he would come to regret.

Relieved and grateful, Darwin thanked Hooker and Lyell for their generous support. He felt that if the greatest botanist and geologist in England – if not Europe – could get behind his theory, it would help break down other people's prejudices. He told Joseph just this.

For the time being, however, those prejudices remained under wraps. Charles now set aside the detailed manuscript he had been working on and began writing up a shorter version for publication as a book. There was no time to waste.

Hooker presents Charles's theory, but doesn't get the reception he, or Charles, expected.

Publication

On the Origin of Species by Means of Natural Selection was finally published in November 1859, despite a few bumps along the way.

At one stage, a horrified Joseph discovered that his children had scribbled over one of the precious manuscripts that Charles had given him to comment on. Hooker sheepishly confessed what had happened to Charles, who luckily knew what children were like and was very understanding, stating, "I have the old manuscript, otherwise the loss would have killed me!"

Hooker's children chose the wrong scrap paper that day!

In another setback, an editor advised Charles that he would get better sales if he cut most of what he had written and made it a book about pigeons! Fortunately, Charles had no intention of taking the editor's advice.

Despite his low expectations, Charles's book was an instant hit. The first edition sold out immediately and others followed as the public lapped it up. It has never been out of print since. Yet, hand in hand with the popularity, came the fury that Charles had been dreading. Many of his friends were unhappy with what he'd written and said cruel things. Others accused Joseph of blindly following Charles. It was criticism of his friend that stung Charles the most. But he need not have minded. Joseph was now convinced that his friend's theory was right and was not afraid to say so, even in public.

Darwin's book was an instant hit and sold out immediately!

Hooker defends Darwin

Thomas Huxley

A month after the book came out, Joseph became the first scientist to put his support for Charles's theory in writing, referring to it in an essay about Australian plants.

A year later, Joseph travelled to Oxford to defend the theory in person, along with naturalist Thomas Huxley, at a debate held by the British Association for the Advancement of Science. Poor Charles was sick and unable to attend.

Samuel Wilberforce

Their opponent was the powerful Bishop of Oxford, Samuel Wilberforce. The fiery bishop was hopping mad at Charles's suggestion that man, beast and plant had evolved from the same simple life form. In his rage, he demanded to know which of Huxley's grandparents was related to an ape. A quick-thinking Huxley replied that he would rather be related to an ape than to a man who used his intelligence to make fun of serious scientific debate.

By now, Joseph's blood was boiling and he was ready to do his worst. Ignoring the boisterous audience, he boldly presented the arguments to rounds of applause.

Charles later admitted that he had been brought to tears on reading about his friend's performance. Few friends could be more loyal or more courageous than Hooker.

Joseph defended his friend.

The evolution of *Origins*

Charles's book was published and
would soon be translated into eleven
different languages, but that was not the
end of the matter.

It was simply the start of another chapter. Charles was the
first to declare that his theory was incomplete. There were always
more questions to answer, criticisms to respond to and gaps to fill in.
With each new edition of the book, Charles made changes and corrections.
In the fifth edition he introduced the phrase, 'survival of the fittest', which is
now used as shorthand for his theory of natural selection.

*Charles made changes to his theory with
each new edition of the book.*

Keen to find more evidence to prove his point and perfect his argument,
Charles ensured Down House remained a storehouse for his many collections
and a giant investigative laboratory. Charles, his children and his staff
experimented on everything from orchids and insect-eating plants to lowly
earthworms. Nobody blinked an eyelid when, on one occasion,
Charles asked his son, Francis, to play his bassoon to some
worms. When the worms failed to respond, Charles put
them in pots and placed them on the piano while
Emma tinkled the keys. It was just
another normal day in the
Darwin household.

*Francis and
Emma serenading
earthworms.*

Darwin's next book

Peahen (female)

In between his experiments, Charles began writing his next major book, in which he tackled the issue of human evolution for the first time.

Until this point, Charles had avoided writing about this sensitive subject in detail. In 1871, however, he declared that, without a doubt, humans had also descended from the very simplest form of life.

Peacock (male)

The book, called *The Descent of Man and Selection in Relation to Sex*, also answered a question that had been bothering Charles: why do males and females of the same species often look so different? It was something that his theory had so far not been able to explain. The animal that particularly frustrated him was the peacock. With his magnificent but seemingly useless tail, the male peacock is very different from the female peahen. Why, Charles wondered, did the peacock have such an elaborate tail when it would surely attract predators in search of a tasty meal?

After much quill chewing, he arrived at the answer. The bigger and better his tail, the more likely a peacock was to attract a peahen to have peachicks with. Therefore, peacock tails had evolved to become increasingly impressive. Charles called this part of his theory 'sexual selection' and he was convinced that it had played a key role in the development of humans too.

Although the book was another roaring success, the newspapers had a field day – printing cartoons of its author depicted as an ape. But Charles was not particularly bothered. In the 12 years since he had published *On the Origin of Species*, his ideas had taken hold amongst many respected thinkers. Bit by bit, he was winning the argument. Spurred on by this thought, he continued with his work – helped by his family and friends.

Charles's second book was a roaring success.

Hooker: Director of Kew Gardens

Meanwhile, Joseph had travelled across the globe, studying and collecting plant life. However, in 1865, it was time for him to come home for good.

Joseph's father had died, and so he was to become Director of the Royal Botanic Gardens, Kew, in his place. It was an enormous task with many moving parts.

As well as keeping the gardens running, Joseph set about expanding Kew's herbarium collections and building its first plant science laboratory. He also worked hard to make Kew one of the world's leading centres of botanical knowledge and expertise.

Joseph's father couldn't have found a better person to take over Kew.

Hooker rises to the top

From his desk at Kew and consulting other scholars around the globe, the strong-minded Joseph made his presence felt. Working alongside fellow botanist, George Bentham, he produced *Genera Plantarum* – a three-volume handbook that described nearly 100,000 species and created a model for plant classification (organising plants into categories) that would be used throughout the British Empire.

Planting around the world

But Joseph was not just interested in categorising. One part of his job involved helping the British Empire make money from plants, such as rubber, coffee and tea. This entailed moving these plants around the world and planting them where they would not naturally be found. We now know how harmful this can be to environments and delicate ecosystems, as well as the livelihoods of local peoples, but back then few people appreciated this – including Joseph. As far as he was concerned, he had a job to do. He even earned himself a knighthood from doing it.

Yet, Joseph did care deeply about protecting the plant kingdom, and a visit to California's magnificent redwood forests in 1877 sparked a desire to save them from destruction by loggers.

Redwood trees can reach 40 metres tall, as high as a thirteen-storey building!

Loyal friends

Amidst all of this, Joseph still found time to help Charles. Using his network of contacts, he ensured that Charles's ideas were discussed and defended around the world. Back in Kew, he carried out experiments on plants to help prove Charles's thinking.

On one of his frequent visits to Down House, he arrived with bunches of stolen government bananas from Kew's greenhouses. They were a rare and exotic treat in Victorian Britain and a kind pick-me-up for a sickly Charles.

Yet, even during his own suffering, Charles was still a vital support to Joseph too. When the Hookers' six-year-old daughter, Minnie, died in 1863, it was to Charles he immediately turned, knowing that he had suffered the same painful loss. So too, when Joseph's wife, Frances, also died in 1874, he looked to Charles for comfort, confiding in him about his feelings of sadness and despair.

Darwin's last days

By now, Charles was growing older and reaching the
final years of his life.

His children had grown up and moved away, and whilst he continued to work
on his projects, he was a shadow of the man who had galloped with gauchos and
chased beetles around rainforests. His life ran like clockwork …

Every day he would
write in his study …

… and stroll around the
Sandwalk with his dog, Polly.

He would take time to talk with
the gardeners in the hothouses …

… and play with his grandson,
Bernard …

… or beat Emma at
backgammon!

And in the evenings he
would go for walks to hear
the nightingales sing.

Charles receives the praise he deserves.

Humble to the end

Happily tucked away in Down House, Darwin seldom ventured far. On one rare visit to London to attend a lecture, he was surprised to hear the audience start clapping as he entered the room. Confused, Charles swivelled around to see whom they were applauding. It was some time before he realised that it was him!

It would be one of the last times he made it to the busy streets of the big city. On 19 April 1882, Charles died from heart failure at home, with Emma at his bedside. Although Emma had planned to bury him in Down (now known as Downe) village parish church, the nation wanted to honour their scientific hero by laying him to rest alongside other great British figures.

Charles's funeral was held with huge fanfare in Westminster Abbey and he was buried in the north aisle of the Abbey's nave, just a few feet away from Sir Isaac Newton. Among the men who carried him there in his coffin was, of course, Joseph Hooker.

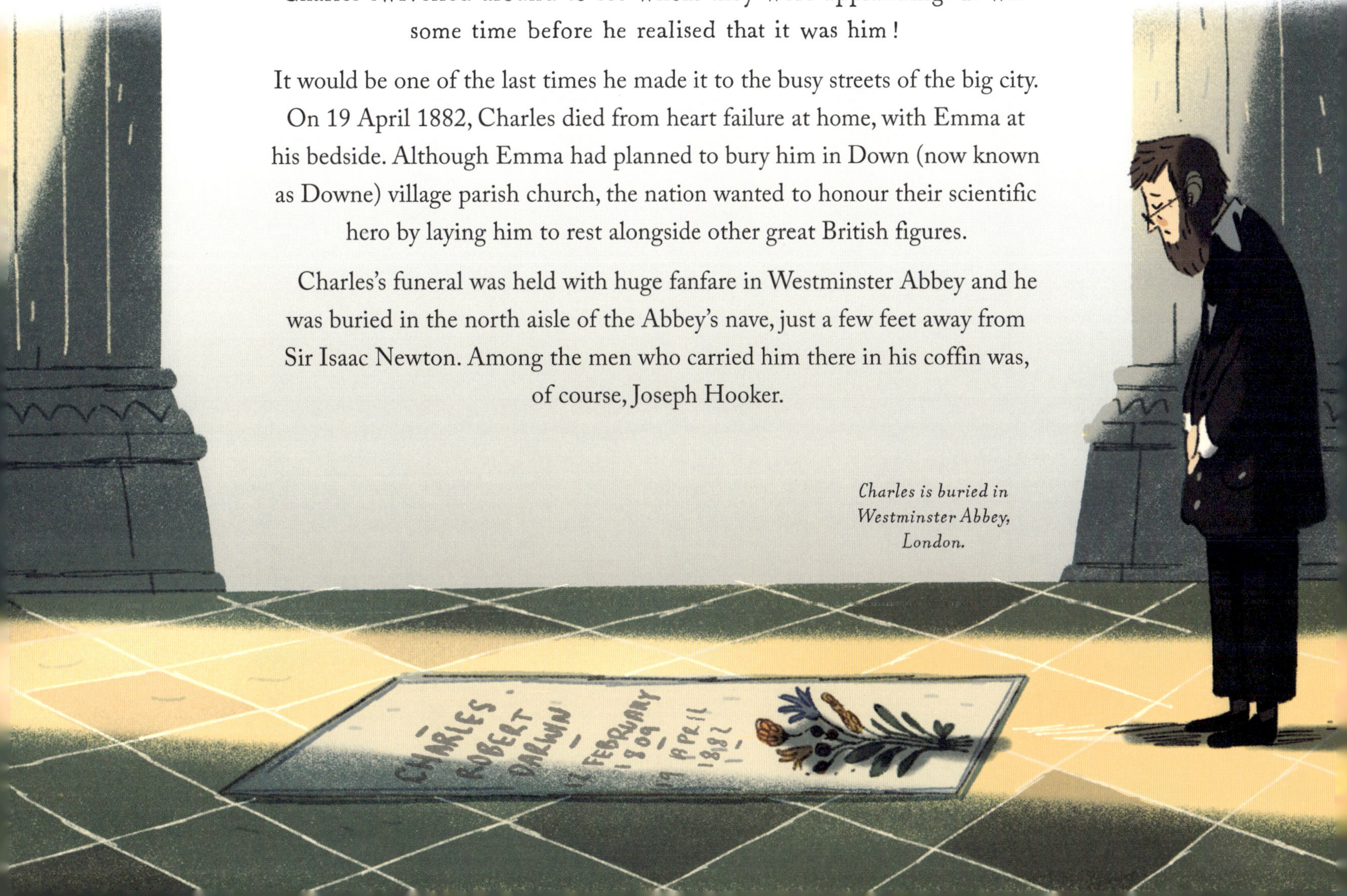

Charles is buried in Westminster Abbey, London.

Hooker's life after Darwin

But whilst Charles's adventure had come to an end, Joseph's would continue for another twenty-nine years.

Joseph had married his second wife, Hyacinth Symonds, in 1876. Hyacinth was the widow of another famous naturalist and the pair went on to have two sons: Joseph and Richard. Now in his sixties and as hard working as ever, Joseph still found time to play with his young sons – getting down on all fours and pretending to be a fierce lion, using his long, shaggy beard as a mane.

Joseph always made time for his family ...

Joseph was sixty-eight when Richard was born, and ready to take life a little slower. Stepping down as Director of Royal Botanic Gardens, Kew, and handing over the reins to his son-in-law, he and his family moved to a large house not too far from London. Here, Joseph spent his days working on his plant collections – dissecting, drawing and identifying them from early in the morning until late at night. Although he had retired from Kew, he would never retire from botany and would continue to collect rewards and honours for his work for years to come.

... though of course, he never stopped working.

72

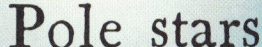

Pole stars

In 1893, showing no signs of slowing down, Joseph began compiling an enormous catalogue of all the known seed plants from around the world.

Called the *Index Kewensis*, this massive project was paid for by Charles, who had left Joseph the money in his will. It is still used by researchers worldwide today to identify and provide scientific plant names, and is a fitting monument to a phenomenal friendship.

So important was that friendship to Joseph, that he later described Charles as his 'pole star'. This is the star traditionally used by sailors to navigate the seas. Coming from a former Royal Naval Officer, it was high praise indeed.

Joseph's own star was still shining brightly when, in 1901, he returned to the University of Glasgow to open its first purpose-built botanical laboratory. Botany was now a respected science, rather than the poor cousin of medicine, and botanists the world over had the hard-working Joseph to thank for helping make that transformation.

However, all stars burn out eventually and, in December 1911, Joseph slipped away in his sleep, at the grand age of ninety-four. Hyacinth Hooker was asked if she wished to bury her husband in Westminster Abbey, near Charles Darwin. Instead, though, she chose to bury him alongside his father in St Anne's Church, just outside the gates of the world-famous Royal Botanic Gardens, Kew. Here he remains, watching over his proudest legacy.

*St Anne's Church,
Kew Green, London*

JOSEPH DALTON
HOOKER

PART FOUR:
Legacy

Hooker's legacy – sowing the seeds for a better future

Today, Kew leads the way in identifying, conserving and researching our planet's plants and fungi.

With unrivalled collections of plant and fungal specimens and a team of over 350 scientists, it works with partners around the world to try to understand and address some of humanity's biggest challenges – from climate change and feeding our growing population to habitat destruction and disease. Some of these challenges Hooker would have been familiar with, others not. However, it is thanks to his energy and the course he plotted as its director, that Kew is uniquely placed to help protect our delicate Tree of Life.

Scientists and horticulturists working at Kew today.

A lot has changed since Kew opened
its doors, but many of the original
plants and buildings still remain,
including the Palm House which
was built between
1844 and 1848.

Yet, as if all this were not enough, we have something even more fundamental to
thank Joseph for: the vital role he played in helping Charles Darwin develop and
defend his theory of evolution by natural selection. But, to understand just how
important this part of Joseph's legacy is, we must acknowledge quite how and why
Charles Darwin's theory was so game-changing …

Darwin's legacy – the door to a new world

Evolution by Natural Selection was revolutionary because it unlocked the secret to life on Earth, explaining how humans and all living things came into existence. It has shaped our thinking ever since.

It is as though, back in 1859, Charles Darwin opened a secret door through which generation after generation of scientists and thinkers have poured, each making vital new discoveries and transforming lives.

Everywhere you look, you can see this in action: in the work of scientists at Kew as they look for ways to protect the world's ecosystems, in our attitude towards animal welfare and even in our approach to understanding psychology (why humans and animals think and act like they do). But perhaps the most dramatic example of how Charles Darwin's theory has informed science and helped change the world, is the story of DNA …

Some of the many incredible people, discoveries and breakthroughs that have come from Darwin's legacy.

DNA and evolution

Building on the work of other genetic scientists, in 1953, Francis Crick and his colleague James Watson, along with researchers Rosalind Franklin and Maurice Wilkins, discovered the structure of one of the building blocks of life: DNA.

DNA, or deoxyribonucleic acid, is the chemical that makes up our genes and it contains all of the instructions that a living thing needs to grow, reproduce and function. Living organisms pass on their own DNA to their offspring when they reproduce, and it is through DNA that characteristics are passed on from one generation to the next.

Crick and Watson's breakthrough solved the riddle of how DNA works and how, over time, changes to the DNA that makes up genes can lead to the creation of new species.

Charles Darwin knew nothing about DNA or genetics, and the puzzle of how features were passed on from parents to children continued to bother him right up until his death.

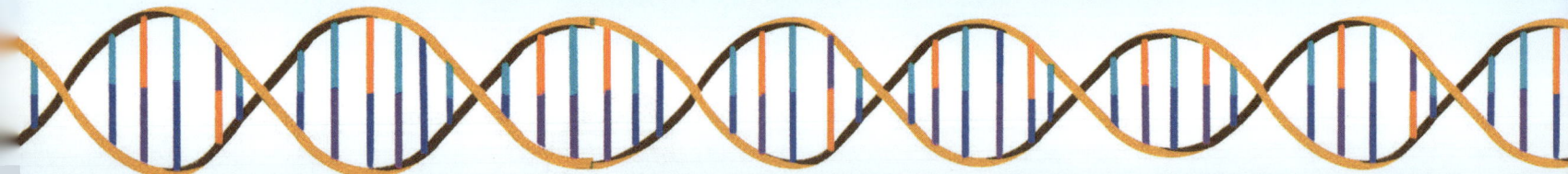

Maurice Wilkins, Rosalind Franklin, James Watson and Francis Crick

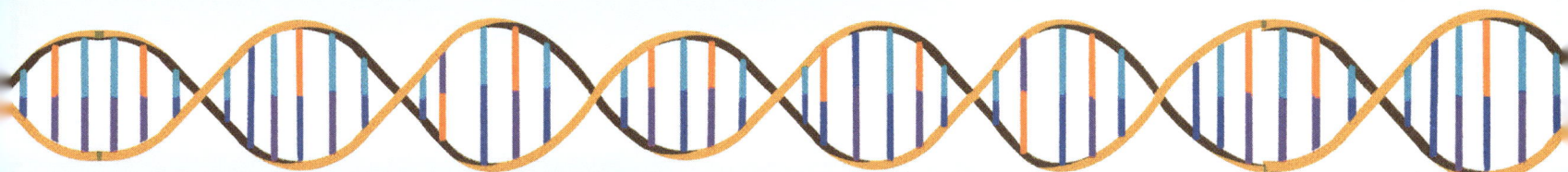

Thanks to the findings of Crick, Watson, Franklin and Wilkins, scientists can compare organisms' DNA to work out how closely they are related to each other. The more similar the DNA, the closer the link. We now know that humans and chimpanzees share 98.8 per cent of their DNA. What's more, we can prove that – as Charles suspected – the Galápagos finches did descend from a single species. We can only imagine how thrilled Charles would have been by all of this. Surely, it is one of the greatest 'I told you so' moments in human history.

No doubt, he would have been even more excited by the ways in which these incredible insights are being put to practical use. Today, DNA can be used to work out family relationships, solve crimes and create disease-resistant crops. Scientists can also use it to work out the likelihood of someone developing diseases, like cancer, and to design more effective medicines and treatments to fight those diseases.

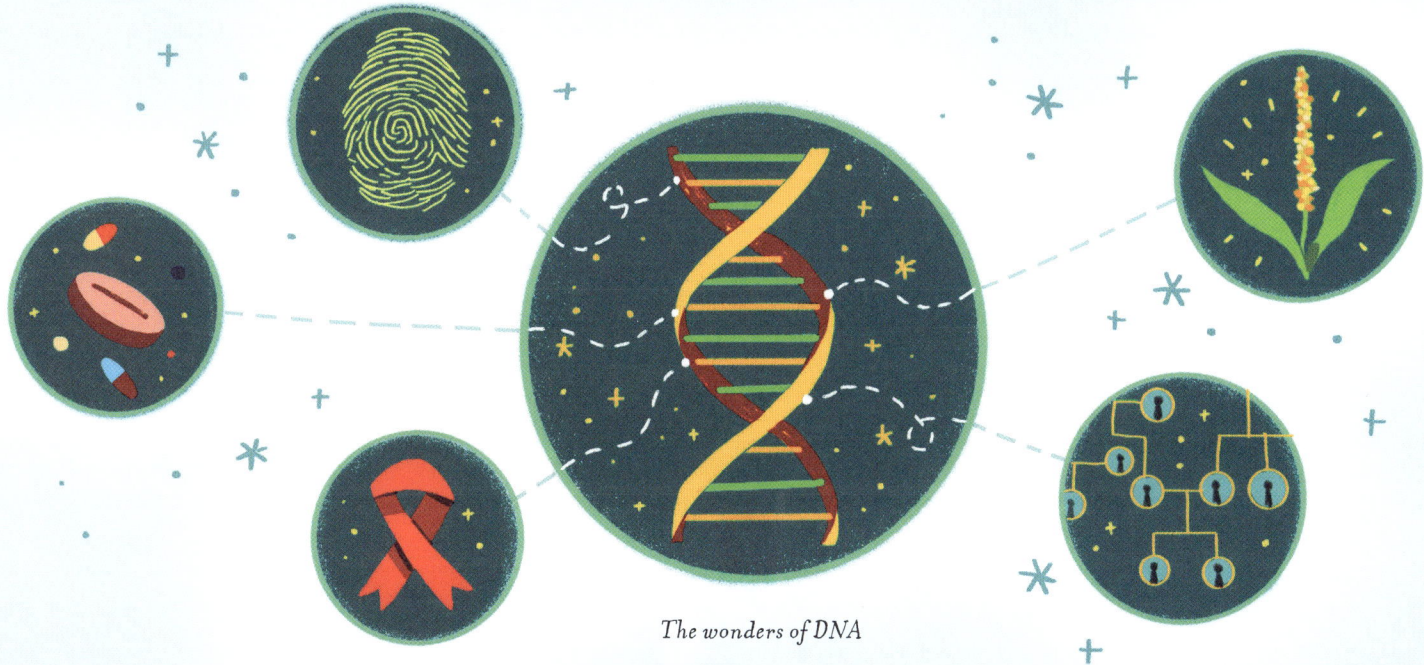

The wonders of DNA

These are just some of the achievements of DNA science and they are just the start. The more scientists understand about genetics, the more they will be able to do. The possibilities are seemingly endless.

Conclusion

All these discoveries - past, present and future - owe something to one man.

A man who had the courage and the dogged determination to seek the truth and to venture where others feared to tread: Charles Darwin. Yet – as our story has shown – just as species were not created in isolation, neither was Charles's theory.

Towards the end of his life, Charles declared that his success depended largely upon his ability to observe and collect facts. He could perhaps have added that most of these facts were collected from, and with the help of, a vast group of men and women from all walks of life.

Charles's triumph, therefore, belongs in part to these people too – the countless family members, friends, colleagues, businessmen, employees, pen pals and casual acquaintances whose help, expert knowledge and friendship he diligently gathered up along the way.

Chief amongst them was, of course, the talented, wise and loyal Joseph Hooker, a man whose friendship was without a doubt one of the most precious things that Charles Darwin collected during his extraordinary life.

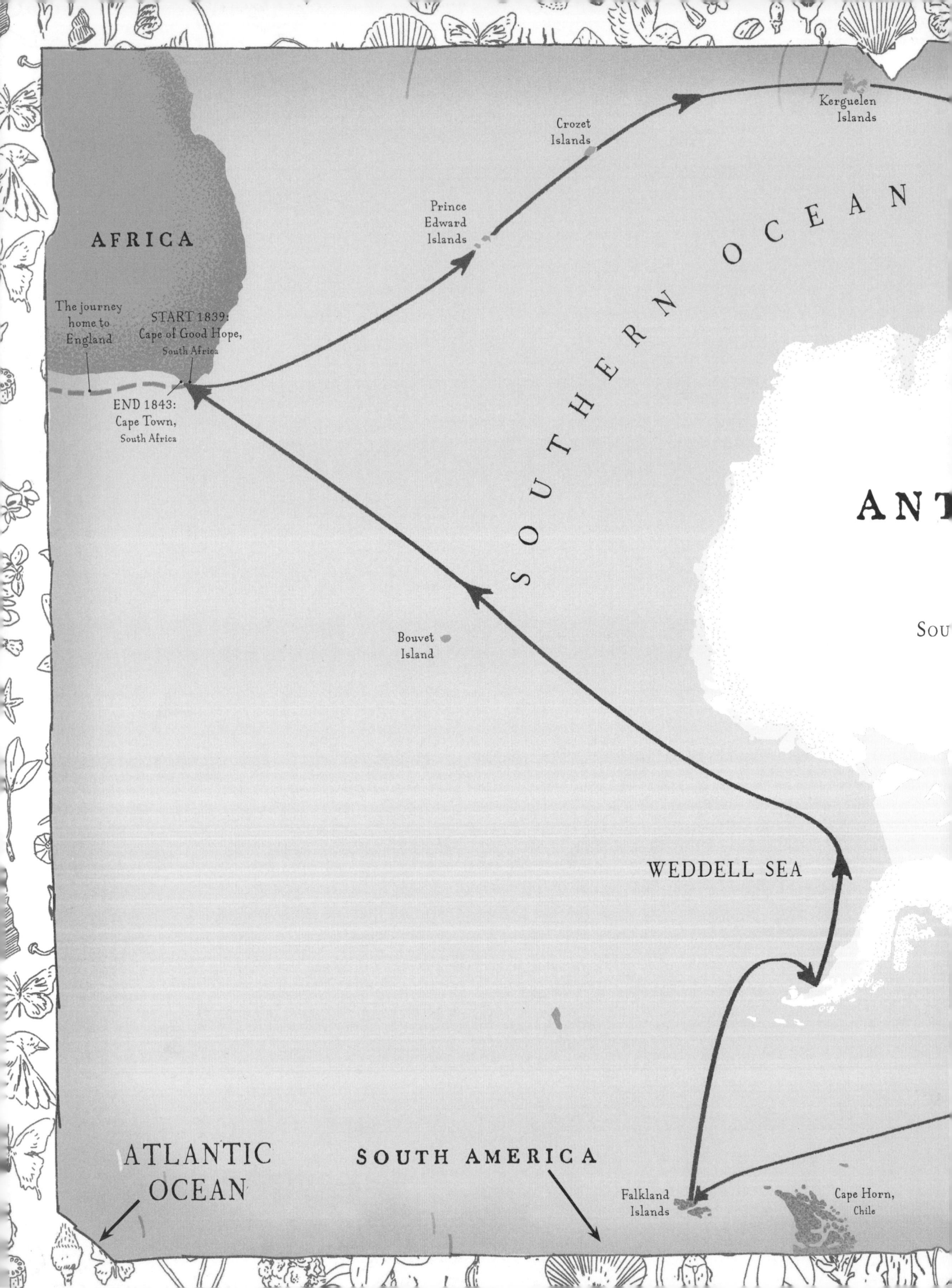

AFRICA

The journey
home to
England

START 1839:
Cape of Good Hope,
South Africa

END 1843:
Cape Town,
South Africa

Prince
Edward
Islands

Crozet
Islands

Kerguelen
Islands

S O U T H E R N   O C E A N

ANT

Sou

Bouvet
Island

WEDDELL SEA

ATLANTIC
OCEAN

SOUTH AMERICA

Falkland
Islands

Cape Horn,
Chile